Harvey Rosen
Jonathan S. Rosen
Present

CVLINARY CARVING
AND PLATE DECORATING

Language Editor: Alyssa S. Eidelberg
Translated By: Alice Ming
Art Director/Graphic Designer: Keffier V. Adkins
Based On: Vegetable Fruit Cutting Carving & Dish Decoration
Chang Wen Liang - Chang Wen Publishing, Ltd.
Yen-chi Chen

International Culinary Consultants
P.O. Box 2202, Elberon, New Jersey 07740 U.S.A.
e-mail: chefharvey@chefharvey.com
web site: http://www.chefharvey.com

ISBN 0-939763-07-9

TABLE OF CONTENTS

CHAPTER 1
The Basics Of Carving

CHAPTER 2
Combination of Shapes and Strips

CHAPTER 3
Floral Carvings

TABLE OF CONTENTS

MESSAGE FROM THE EDITORS

We proudly present "Culinary Carving and Plate Decorating".
Our book introduces and beautifully illustrates the Chinese style
of food decorating and provides readers with the knowledge
to create masterpieces with fruits and vegetables.
We thank Chang Wen Liang for making it possible for us to bring the Chinese art
of vegetable and fruit carving and plate decorating to the English speaking world.
"Culinary Carving and Plate Decorating" illustrates the techniques of
Chinese food carving and plate decorating. Mastering these techniques
will allow you to create the beautiful garnishes and plate decorations
that appear throughout the book.

Chef Harvey Rosen   Chef Jonathan S. Rosen

INTRODUCTION

This book illustrates the grace and beauty of one of the world's most impressive but least known art forms: vegetable and fruit carving. Many of the edible delicacies we enjoy today have a history reaching back to ancient China. In fact, we credit China with developing one of the world's foremost cuisines, and China's culinary influence on the world has continued for thousands of years.

The art form of vegetable and fruit carving emerged from the culinary developments taking place in ancient China. The practice of preparing garnishes to enrich the overall beauty of a meal began during the Tang Dynasty, from 618 to 906 A.D., and continued throughout the Sung Dynasty, which lasted from 960 to 1279 A.D. The public-at-large, however, rarely experienced this lovely and gentle art form because the practice was reserved primarily for the preparation of royal banquets and for the enjoyment of imperial guests.

In today's diet-conscious world, the appearance as well as the contents of the foods we consume assume great significance. Trendy restaurants and culinary magazines alike stress the equal importance of the style and substance of food. Society's ever-increasing interest in health and fitness has heightened our awareness of what we eat, how we eat it, and what it looks like. Healthy and nutritious food can be presented in an appetizing and appealing manner, thus encouraging us to savor what we eat as we admire what we see on our plates!

Although members of the royal family and other aristocrats in ancient China were once the only ones fortunate enough to view the gracious art of vegetable and fruit carving, today the splendor of this art has become accessible to us all. These days, when attending a luncheon, a family dinner, or a holiday banquet, chances are that we will see some type of vegetable or fruit carving or decoration accompanying the meal — because anything beautiful to see and delicious to eat will be admired and enjoyed by all.

The vegetable and fruit carvings and garnishes introduced in this book play a major role in the art of food sculpture. Carvings and garnishes decorate dishes, complement the food, and even help hide any defects in the appearance of the dish.

▦ Arrange garnishes symmetrically on the plate. Garnishes should complement not overwhelm the dish. Usually, a garnish should be placed on both sides or in one corner of the plate, forming a diagonal arrangement. Also, a garnish can be placed in the center of the plate, with the food surrounding the garnish, creating a symmetrical and colorful arrangement. In addition, do not cover more than one quarter of the plate with the garnish, because doing so will tend to reduce the importance of the food itself.

▦ Hot or cold dishes can be decorated with a garnish arranged in flat or on upright arrangement. Several approaches may be taken when decorating a hot dish. You can place the garnish at the center of the plate, and place the food around the garnish. Or, you can place the garnish standing upright at the center or the edge of the plate (for a larger-sized work). You can also decorate a dish by using a garnishing tool to create small garnishes, and then by arranging the pieces around the edge of the plate. While the first arrangement may be most suitable for dishes without a great deal of sauce, the second two arrangements may be used to decorate almost any hot dish.

In general, the size and form of a garnish must suit the purpose or theme of the party for which you prepare the dish.

Roots and stems of vegetables and fruits can be utilized for carving.
The following guidelines should be followed when choosing the material.
The material should be: (1) tender, but not too soft; (2) solid; and (3) colorful.
The materials you select depend upon the design you wish to achieve.
The following, however, are suggestions of materials appropriate for carving:

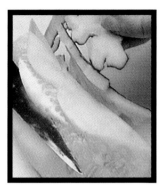

CUCUMBER:
For a flat carving with relief detail, a cucumber makes an excellent choice, especially for the well known "cucumber cup" carving. Choose a cucumber with a regular shape, dense in mass, and fairly ripe (70% ripe or better).

RAMBUTAN:
This exotic fruit is originally from Malaysia and Indonesia. Prior to working with this fruit, always thoroughly clean the fruit with soap and water.

WATERMELON:
For birds and animal carvings, watermelon makes an excellent choice. Watermelon also makes great containers, such as the "watermelon boat" or "basket." Select a watermelon with a trim shape, blackish-green rind, and dense mass.

DURIAN:
Known for its characteristic aroma, this unique fruit, indigenous to Southeast Asia, is rich in minerals, protein, and fat.

PUMPKIN:
Two kinds of pumpkin shapes exist for your use in carving. A spherical shape, used for a "pumpkin cup" or "basket," or a cylindrical shape, best for carving birds and boats.

FIRE DRAGON MELON:
This unusual melon is a hot fruit and should be eaten with cool foods.

MANGOSTEEN:
The "Queen Fruit of the Tropics" from Thailand, Indonesia, and the Philippines. Its dark purple rind and white flesh make it an attractive fruit to use in garnishing and decorating.

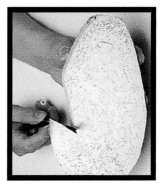

TARO ROOT:
Originally from India and Southeast Asia, this root is an excellent medium for carving because the firm texture is suitable for intricate designs.

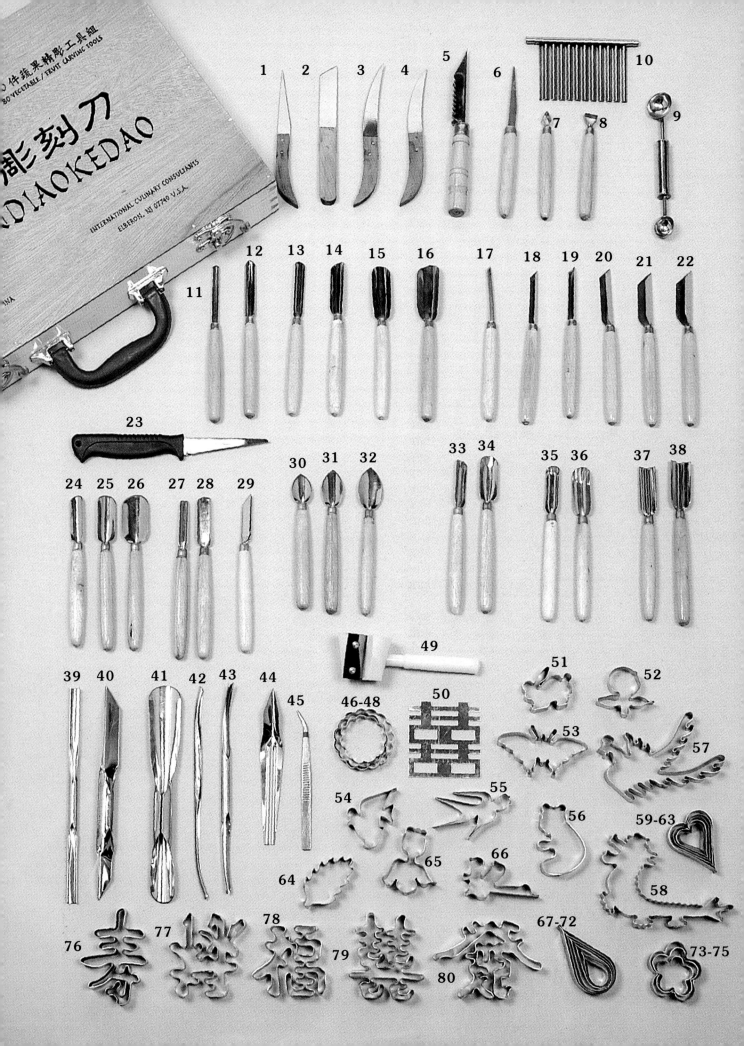

80 Vegetable/Fruit Carving Tools
*Indicates Tools Included In 22 Piece Set

I.C.C. Ref. #	Key #	Description
K-1	1	* Pointed Paring Knife
K-2	2	* Slanted Knife
K-3	3	* Curved Paring Knife
K-4	4	* Bird's Beak Knife
V-1	5	* Fruit/Vegetable Decorator
S-1	6	* Fruit/Vegetable Saw
SP-1	7	* Stripper-Pointed
SF-1	8	* Stripper-Flat
DSS	9	* Double Sided Vegetable/Fruit Scoop
C-1	10	* Crinkle Cutter
U-1	11	* "U" Carving Tool W/Handle
U-2	12	* "U" Carving Tool W/Handle
U-3	13	* "U" Carving Tool W/Handle
U-4	14	* "U" Carving Tool W/Handle
U-5	15	* "U" Carving Tool W/Handle
U-6	16	* "U" Carving Tool W/Handle
V-1	17	* "V" Carving Tool W/Handle
V-2	18	* "V" Carving Tool W/Handle
V-3	19	* "V" Carving Tool W/Handle
V-4	20	* "V" Carving Tool W/Handle
V-5	21	* "V" Carving Tool W/Handle
V-6	22	* "V" Carving Tool W/Handle
K-5	23	Utility Knife
SUS	24	Shallow "U" Small W/Handle
SUM	25	Shallow "U" Med. W/Handle
SUL	26	Shallow "U" Large W/Handle
FBS	27	Flat Bottom Small "U" W/Handle
FBL	28	Flat Bottom Large "U" W/Handle
RV	29	Reversed "V" With Handle
PSS	30	Pointed Spoon Small W/Handle
PSM	31	Pointed Spoon Medium W/Handle
PSL	32	Pointed Spoon Large W/Handle
FSS	33	Flouted Single Small W/Handle
FSL	34	Flouted Single Large W/Handle
MFCS	35	Multi-Flouted Small W/Handle
MFCL	36	Multi-Flouted Large W/Handle
WS	37	Waved Small With Handle
WL	38	Waved Large With Handle
DSFU	39	Double Sided Flat Bottom "U"
DSV	40	Double Sided Large "V"

I.C.C. Ref. #	Key #	Description
DSU	41	Double Sided Large "U"
DSCU	42	Double Sided Curved "U"
DSCV	43	Double Sided Curved "V"
AV	44	Angled "V"
T	45	Tweezers
S-C1	46	Scalloped Cutter 1
S-C2	47	Scalloped Cutter 2
S-C3	48	Scalloped Cutter 3
CS	49	Carrot Shaver
DHT	50	Double Happiness Template
R-C	51	Rabbit Cutter
RF-C	52	Rounded Flower Cutter
BU-C	53	Butterfly Cutter
DO-C	54	Dove Cutter
FD-C	55	Flying Dove Cutter
BE-C	56	Bear Cutter
DR-C	57	Dragon Cutter
P-C	58	Phoenix Cutter
H-C1	59	Heart Cutter 1
H-C2	60	Heart Cutter 2
H-C3	61	Heart Cutter 3
H-C4	62	Heart Cutter 4
H-C5	63	Heart Cutter 5
L-C	64	Leave Cutter
TF-C	65	Tulip Flower Cutter
G-C	66	Goose Cutter
TD-C1	67	Tear Drop Cutter 1
TD-C2	68	Tear Drop Cutter 2
TD-C3	69	Tear Drop Cutter 3
TD-C4	70	Tear Drop Cutter 4
TD-C5	71	Tear Drop Cutter 5
TD-C6	72	Tear Drop Cutter 6
F-C1	73	Flower Cutter 5 Scallops 1
F-C2	74	Flower Cutter 5 Scallops 2
F-C3	75	Flower Cutter 5 Scallops 3
CC-C1	76	Chinese Character (Long Life)
CC-C2	77	Chinese Character (Happiness)
CC-C3	78	Chinese Character (Wealth)
CC-C5	79	Chinese Character (Double Happiness)
CC-C4	80	Chinese Character (Get Rich)

KNIVES

Lubricate the sharpening stone
with water or oil.
Hold the blade of the knife
at a 10 to 20 degree angle
and draw the cutting edge
of the blade against the stone
alternating, first
on one side of the blade
and then the other.
As the blade becomes sharper,
use less pressure.

V-SHAPED CARVING TOOL

Lubricate the sharpening stone
with water or oil. Sharpen the
V-shaped carving tool blade
by placing the tool against the
sharpening stone at a 20 to 25
degree angle. Sharpen each side
of the blade by moving the blade
horizontally, from right to left.
When finished sharpening
the outer surface, smooth out
the inside surface of the blade by
gently moving the tool along
the edge of the sharpening stone.
Use the same method to
sharpen each V-shaped carving
tool, regardless of the size.

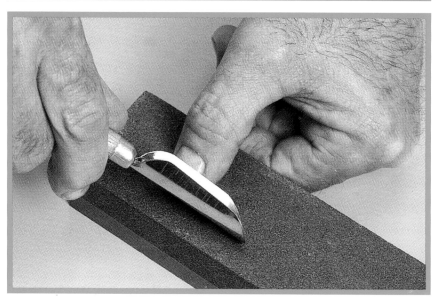

U-SHAPED CARVING TOOL

Lubricate the sharpening stone
with water or oil. To sharpen the
U-shaped carving tool blade,
place the tool against the
sharpening stone at a 20 to 25
degree angle and rotate the tool,
clockwise and then
counter-clockwise as shown.
When finished sharpening
the outer surface, smooth out
the inside surface of the blade by
gently rotating the tool along
the edge of the sharpening stone.
Use the same method to
sharpen each U-shaped carving
tool, regardless of the size.

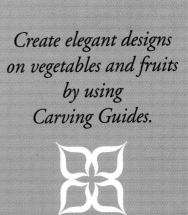

*Create elegant designs
on vegetables and fruits
by using
Carving Guides.*

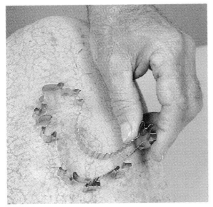

❶ Place the carving guide, as flat as possible, against the side of a melon.

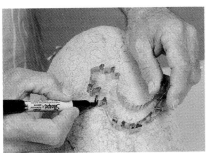

❷ Trace the shape of the guide with a marker. Cut along the outline of the shape to create beautiful designs.
Use the V-shaped carving tool to decorate the background of the designs.

1. Turtle **2.** Lobster **3.** Butterfly **4.** Dragon **5.** Crab **6.** Bird
7. Parrot **8.** Goldfish **9.** Fish **10.** Tulip **11.** Flower **12.** Dragon **13.** Phoenix

❶ Hold the cutter at right angles to the side of the vegetable and push in to form the design. Cut a slice from the side where you have formed the design. Carefully remove the design from the slice. For an inlaid effect, use vegetables of contrasting colors.

For additional instructions and plate decorating suggestions, see page 22.

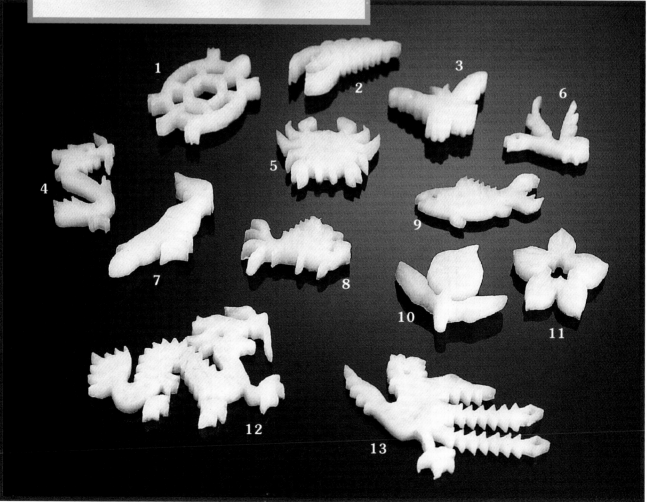

The Double Happiness character is an ancient Chinese symbol depicted in many paintings and carvings of China. The symbol is a welcome expression wherever it is displayed. Now, you can easily add this good wish to your fruit and vegetable carvings.

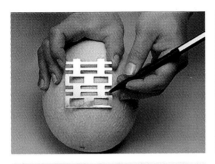

❶ Create the double happiness character design by placing the template against the side of a melon. Trace the shape of the double happiness template with a marker.

❷ Cut along the outline of the character with a paring knife. Remove the excess rind from around the character.

❸ To achieve a deeper, more pronounced, double happiness character design: Use the paring knife or carving tool to cut into the melon flesh removing all of the excess rind and some of the flesh to achieve the desired effect.

Gherkin Arrangement

#1

Materials...Gherkin, Maraschino Cherry

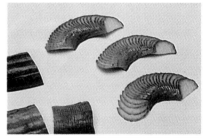

Gherkin Arrangement

#2

Materials...Gherkin, Maraschino Cherry

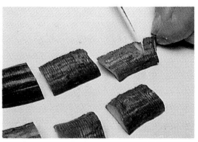

❶ Cut each lengthwise half of a gherkin into sections. Make a series of thin slices on each section, but leave one edge attached.

❷ The attached edges form the base for making the slices into a fan shape. With a light touch, separate the slices to create the fan shape.

Gherkin Arrangement

#3

Materials...Gherkin, Orange, Maraschino Cherry

❶ Select a fresh gherkin cucumber with a straight shape. Wash and cut the gherkin into thin slices.

❷ Use three slices and arrange the slices into a triangle. Place each triangle along the edge of a plate. Use a light colored plate to best display the garnish.

❸ Place half a maraschino cherry in the center of each triangle.

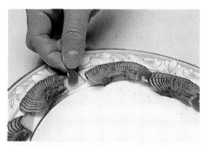

❸ Place half a maraschino cherry between each section. Arrange on the edge of a circular or oval plate.

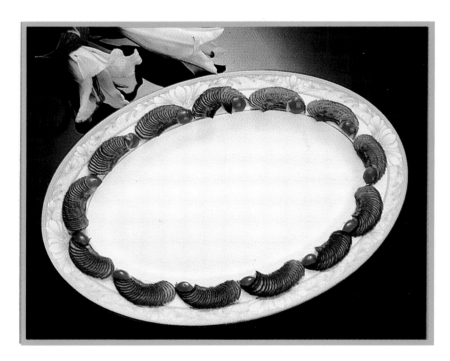

❶ Select a fresh and brightly colored orange. Cut it into thin slices.

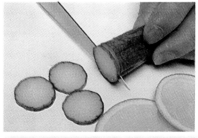

❷ Select a fresh gherkin and cut the gherkin into thin slices crosswise.

❸ Set these slices of gherkin on a base slice of orange, then place half a marachino cherry on top for a pretty combination of colors.

15

❶ Select a fresh and brightly colored orange and cut it into thin slices crosswise.

❷ Make a slice from the center to the edge of the orange slice.

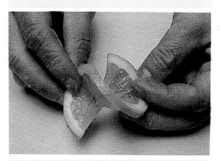

❸ Twist the orange slice as shown in the photograph.

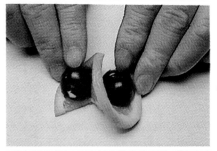

❹ Place a maraschino cherry on each side of the twisted piece of orange and put a small broccoli floret along the sides of the garnish.

Cucumber, Orange Combination Arrangement

Materials... Orange, Cucumber

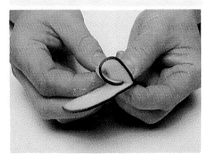

❶ Select a fresh cucumber with a straight shape, and cut it in half lengthwise.

❷ Cut a series of double slices by making a thin slice crosswise, but do not cut through the cucumber. Next, make a slice which cuts through the cucumber.

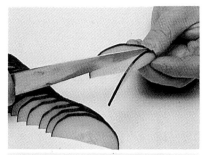

❸ Then, once again make a thin slice which does not cut through the cucumber. Repeat the process.

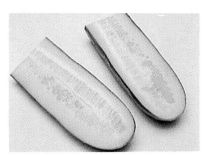

❹ Fold the upper piece of the slice into the crease, forming a curve.

❺ First arrange the orange slices on the edge of a plate. Next, arrange the tucked "double slices" of cucumber at the inner edge of the orange slices.

Greens

Materials... Mustard Greens, Maraschino Cherry

❶ Select the central green part of a mustard green. Cook the greens in boiling water, and then rinse them in cold water.

❷ Slice a center stalk of mustard green lengthwise to make long strips for stems.

❸ Prepare another center stalk to become a "double open."

❹ Make a "double open" by diagonally cutting the piece of stalk, but do not cut through the stalk. Make a second cut crosswise above the previous cut; this time, cut through the stalk.

❺ Repeat instruction 4. Place the opened "double opens" in a plate to form leaves and petals as shown. Decorate with maraschino cherries as flower buds.

Cucumber Fancy Arrangement #1

Materials... Cucumber, Radish

❶ Select a fresh white radish and cut it lengthwise into a pentagonal (five-sided) shape.

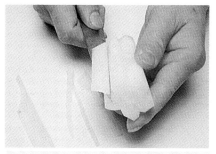

❷ Cut a groove at the center of each side to form a flower shape.

❸ Using a spiral-like cut, turn the knife two times around the vegetable to form a beautiful blossom.

❹ As shown on page 17, create a tucked "double slice." Arrange the tucked "double slices" along the edge of a plate, then fill in the decoration with the radish blossoms.

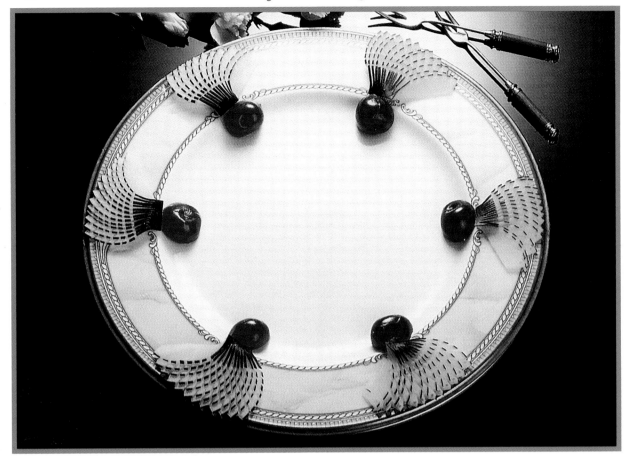

Cucumber Fancy Arrangement #2

Materials... Cucumber, Maraschino Cherry

❶ Select a fresh cucumber. Cut a section approximately 1/2"-3/4" in length, and quarter it lengthwise.

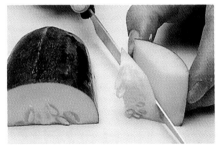

❷ Cut the seeds out of the cucumber.

❸ Score the skin of each piece. Cut each quarter crosswise into thin slices, leaving one edge attached.

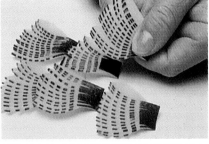

❹ Gently open the slices to make fans, and arrange them along the edge of a plate. Set half a maraschino cherry in front of each fan.

Cucumber Fancy Arrangement #3

Materials... Cucumber

❶ Select a fresh cucumber with a straight shape. Cut it lengthwise into quarters. Cut out the seeds.

❷ Cut the quartered cucumbers diagonally into thin slices, leaving one edge attached.

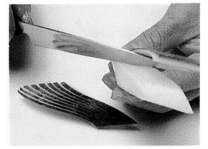

❸ Using a thin knife, cut the skin back from the quarter of a cucumber, but leave the skin attached at the edge.

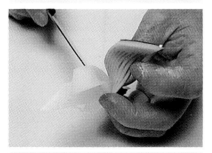

❹ Cut a second layer under the skin. That is, after first cutting back the skin, then cut a layer of flesh, leaving the layer attached at the edge.

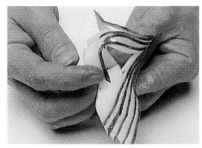

❺ Holding the quartered cucumber in one hand, use your other hand to open the thin slices and fold them into the crease one piece at a time.

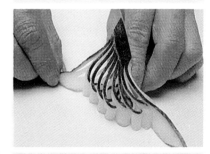

❻ Finish the garnish as displayed. Decorate with carved blossoms.

Happiness And Longevity

Materials...
Carrot, Cucumber

❶ Select a fresh, large carrot. Wash and cut off the top of the carrot.

❷ Using your palm, press the cutter into the cut-off side of the carrot.

❸ Remove the cutter. The design will show in the carrot.

❹ Cut the carrot crosswise into thin slices. Place the design slices along the outer edge of the plate.
(See page 12 for other design cutters.)

❶ Cut 11/2" of a cucumber lengthwise. Score the skin of the cucumber section, and then cut it into slices of "double open" (see page 18).

❷ Open each slice of "double open" to form a petal. Arrange five "petals" to shape the first layer of the blossom.

❸ Arrange another five "petals" in between the first layer of petals, forming a complete blossom.

❹ Place a maraschino cherry on top of the blossom center, and then arrange the blossoms and leaves to complete your design.

Floral Arrangement

Materials...Cucumber, Maraschino Cherry

23

Chapter 1 · The Basics Of Carving

Yellow Rose

Materials...
Pickled Takuruan

❶ Wash and dry a piece of pickled takuruan. Cut it crosswise into thin slices.

❷ Roll up a slice of pickled takuruan to make a flower center and hold it in your hand.

❸ Add slices of takuruan clockwise around the center to form the petals of the rose.

❹ Use a total of twelve slices of takuruan to form a rose blossom. Open each "petal" gently for the best display of the blossom.

Rose

Materials...
Carrot

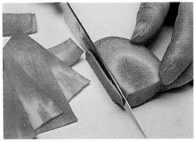

❶ Select a large, fresh carrot. Cut the carrot into thin slices 1" x 2" in length.

❷ Soak the slices in salty water to soften. Fold the softened slices in half, on the diagonal.

❸ Roll up a piece of folded carrot to form the flower's center.

❹ Fold three slices in half diagonally, and set these slices around the flower center at the first row of petals.

❺ Repeat this same procedure to make several rows of petals, alternating the position of the petals between rows.

Tomato Arrangement #1

Materials... Tomato

❶ Select a ripe, bright firm tomato. Wash the tomato and cut it into quarters.

❷ Cut each quarter of tomato into three slices lengthwise.

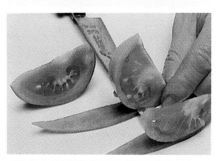

❸ Using a thin-blade knife, cut a layer of tomato skin from one end, but leave the skin attached on the other end.

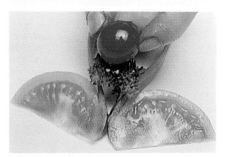

❹ Place two slices end to end, creating a "bunny ear" effect with the layer of skin. Arrange other tomato slices around the plate.

Tomato Arrangement #2

Materials... Tomato

❶ Wash a fresh firm tomato. Cut the tomato into quarters, and then cut each quarter into three lengthwise slices.

❷ Using a thin-blade knife, cut a layer of tomato skin from one end, but leave the skin attached on the other end.

❸ Fold the opened rind into the crease. Arrange the slices clockwise on the edge of a plate. Set maraschino cherries and broccoli florets between each slice.

Tomato Arrangement #3

Materials... Tomato

❶ Wash a fresh firm tomato.
Cut the tomato in half, then cut each
half into three lengthwise slices.

❷ Using the point of a knife, cut a
V-shaped wedge into the skin of the
slice.

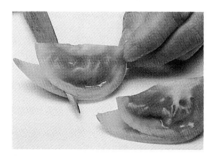

❸ Hold the tomato so that the point of the
V faces left. Cut a layer of skin from right
to left, leaving the skin attached
at the end of the slice.

❹ Pull back the layer of skin and prop up
the point of the V against the flesh of the
tomato slice.

❺ Arrange the blossom on a plate, and
use "double open" slices of gherkin
(see page 14) to form the stem.

Narcissus

Materials...
Cucumber, Orange, Garlic Clove

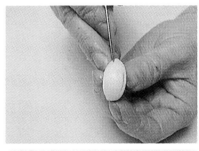

❶ Wash a clove of garlic.

❷ Using a thin blade knife, carefully cut thin pieces of petal into the clove.

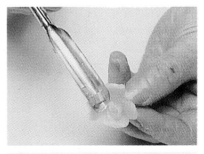

❸ Carefully peel back the skin.

❹ As shown, separate each petal using the point of a knife.

❺ Decorate the flower with a sliver of carrot at the center.

Taro

*Materials... Taro Root,
Broccoli Floret, Oranges*

❶ Cut the rind off a taro root, and then rinse the taro. Cut the taro crosswise into a cylinder about two inches in length.

❷ Serrate the piece of the taro.

❸ With the point of a sharp knife, cut the taro at a 45 degree angle. Use a spiral-like cut, turning the knife three times around the vegetable. (see pg. 19)

❹ Using your hands, turn an end of the taro to form a blossom.

❺ Use the three taro blossoms to form a triple combination.

❻ Place a piece of cherry at the center of the flower. Place the taro triple blossom at various points on a dish. Arrange the triple blossoms with semi-circle slices of oranges.

Daisy

Materials...
Scallions

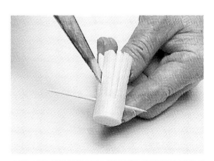

❶ Select a light green section of a scallion. Cut the scallion lengthwise into a three inch piece.

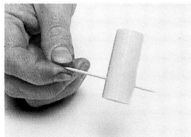

❷ Insert a toothpick one inch above the bottom of the scallion piece, through the center of the scallion.

❸ Using a knife with a thin blade, cut the scallion lengthwise into even strips. Do not cut through the other end of the scallion.

❹ A close-up of the scallion "flower" looking down.

❺ Open the "petals." Arrange overlapping slices of cucumber and carrots at the edge of a plate, and place a broccoli floret under the "daisy" for contrast.

A Double
Happiness Has
Descended Upon
The Home

Materials...
Cucumber

❶ Sketch a design on the skin of the cucumber. Carve out the picture with a knife. You may use a stencil to trace the design.

❷ Complete carving the design.

❸ Cut away the flesh behind the raised design. The beauty of this garnish is enhanced by the color contrast.

❹ Use the flesh to create a rock for the background.

Happiness Has Filled A Golden Cup

Materials... Pumpkin

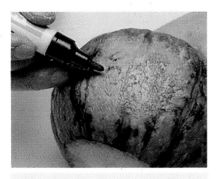

❶ Using a marker, sketch a design on the pumpkin. You may use a stencil to trace the design.

❷ Carve the outline of the design.

❸ To make the design more pronounced, carve out the spaces within and around the design.

Legacies Of Chinese Opera

Materials...
Eggs, Pumpkin

❶ Using a pin, poke a small hole at the top center of a cleaned egg. Drain out the egg white and yolk.

❷ Draw a circumference lengthwise with a marker to divide the eggshell into two halves.

❸ Sketch a Chinese Opera singer's face on the eggshell.

❹ Vary the color and picture to suit your taste.

Snowmen

Materials...
Eggs

❶ Shell a cooked egg, and cut off each end of the egg.

❷ Cut a slice crosswise at the large end of the egg.

❸ Attach the slice to the pointed end of the egg. String these pieces together with a toothpick and place a quail egg on top.

❹ Attach a steamed black mushroom on top of the quail egg, forming a snowman.

❺ Add small pieces of cherry for the snowman's cheeks, eyes, nose, and buttons.

Jasmine Facing Heaven

Materials...
Chili Pepper

❶ Select a bright and straight chili pepper. Cut petals on the pepper.

❷ Trim the petals and remove the excess pepper.

❸ Cut the seeds out from the pepper.

❹ Open the petals gently to form a jasmine flower. Decorate with cucumber and shreds of daikon.

Hibiscus

Materials...
Taro Root, Carrot

❶ Cut a carrot into a cylinder with a diameter of approximately 1".

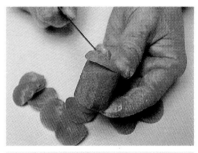

❷ Cut the carrot cylinder crosswise into thin curved slivers. Five slices make up one group of petals.

❸ Using a V-shaped carving tool, score strips on a small round piece of taro which will be used as the flower center.

❹ Glue five petals to the taro center to form a blossom.

❺ Glue a second layer of petals to make a fuller blossom. Decorate with greens, such as cucumber slices.

Jasmine

Materials... Daikon, Carrot

❶ Carve a daikon into pieces in the shape of tear drops.

❷ Cut the daikon pieces crosswise into thin curved slices which will form petals.

❸ Score a small stick of carrot which will form a flower center. Glue the petals to the flower center.

❹ Glue a second layer of petals in between the first layer of petals.

White Rose

Materials... Daikon

❶ Select a fresh white daikon. Cut off the end with the stem, and keep the end with the root.

❷ Cut a section of daikon approximately 1 1/2" in length. Cut off five wedges from the piece, leaving the shape of a blossom.

❸ Make a deep cut on each of the five sides, separating the first layer of petals from the center.

❹ Cut at an angle between the petals and the center section, forming a rim of petals. Remove the excess.

❺ Repeat instruction #3 and #4.

❼ Cut six layers of petals in this manner. A white rose will appear.

Yellow Blossom Of Oleander

Materials... Pumkin, Taro Root

❶ Using a small piece of taro, make a flower center.

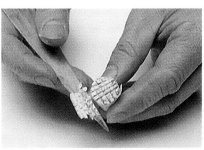

❷ Cut a piece of pumpkin flesh into a heart-shaped cylinder.

❸ Cut the pumpkin piece crosswise into thin slices. Eight slices make up one group of petals.

❹ Holding the flower center, glue a group of petals onto the flower center one by one.

Yellow Locust Blossom

Materials... Taro, Cucumber, Green Leaves

❶ Cut a taro into three heart-shaped pieces. Carve each piece so that you form one thin, one medium, and one thick piece.

❷ Trim one side of each piece into a jagged shape.

❸ Cut the taro pieces crosswise into thin curved slices. Five identical slices form one group of petals.

❹ Form a small piece of carrot into a stick, and score its surface to form a flower center.

❺ Glue petals into the flower center, one group forms one layer of petals.

❻ Arrange each layer so that the smaller sized petals are closer to the center.

Chapter 2 · Combining Shapes & Strips

Zinnias

Materials... Yam, Taro Root

Magnolia

Materials... Radish, Carrot

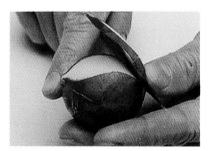

❶ Cut a radish lengthwise into curved thin slices. Three identical slices form a group, and one group makes a layer of petals.

❷ Score a stick of carrot to make a flower center and glue petals around the center.

❸ Three layers of petals form a blossom, with smaller sized petals around the center.

❶ Cut a yam into pieces 3/4" thick.

❷ Carve the pieces into a willow leaf shape.

❸ Make a jagged edge on each side of the leaf.

❹ Cut thin curved slices.

❺ Carve a small piece of taro into cylinder. Score the surface of the taro to form a flower center.

❻ Cut a circular groove along the flower center.

❼ Ten slices of yam make up one group of petals. Glue one group of petals into the groove of the flower center.

❽ Glue a second layer of petals which are smaller than the petals of the first layer.

❾ Repeat the procedure. Three layers of petals is usually adequate to form the zinnia.

Magnolia

Materials...
Radish, Carrot

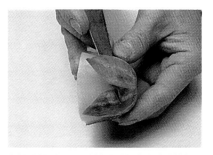

② Carve petals from the cucumber end. Carve the skin from behind the petals. Remove the excess skin.

③ Cut the petals back from the flesh carefully, so that the bottom of the petals remains attached.

④ Carve a second layer of petals, decreasing the size of the petals from the outer edge to the center.

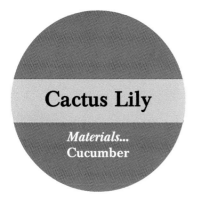

Cactus Lily

Materials...
Cucumber

① Cut off each end of a cucumber. These ends will form blossoms.

⑤ The layers will form a lotus-like blossom. Decorate the blossom center with small wild flowers.

Red Pompom

Materials... Carrot, Gherkin

❶ Cut a carrot into a cylinder. Cut a thin slice from around the cylinder forming a strip.

❷ Prepare a bowl of salt water to soak the carrot strip.

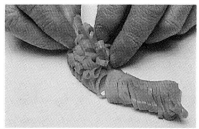

❸ Soak the carrot strip in salty water until it becomes soft and pliable so that it can be folded.

❹ Lay the carrot strip flat. Fold lengthwise.

❺ Slice even thin strips on the folded edge, leaving the opposite edge intact.

❻ Roll up to form a beautiful pompom.

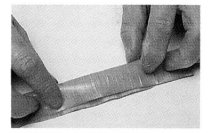

❼ Cut a gherkin into the shape of branches and leaves and arrange to complete the garnish.

Chrysanthemum

Materials... Carrot, Baby Corn

❶ Cut a circular groove 1/2" below the large end of a baby corn.

❷ Carve a piece of carrot into the shape of a long thin petal.

❸ Cut a groove lengthwise at one end of the carrot piece to form a V shape.

❹ Cut the carrot piece crosswise into thin curved slices.

❺ Glue each petal into the groove of the baby corn, with the V-shaped tip of the petals facing the outside.

❻ Ten petals make up one layer, and three layers make a blossom.

Improvisation #1

Materials...
Cucumber

❶ Cut the center section of a large cucumber crosswise into 1" thick slices.

❷ Cut one end from each slice.

❸ Make a V cut across the skin of the cucumber about 1/2" from the bottom.

❹ Make another V cut on the skin to make a W shape.

❺ Cut the skin from the flesh of the cucumber, but leave the last 1/2" of skin attached.

❻ Lift the skin up away from the flesh.

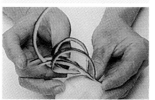

❼ Tuck the end slices of skin into the area where the skin remains attached to the flesh.

❽ Repeat steps #5 through #7 to complete two additional slices.

❾ Tuck the ends of these slices one by one.

❶ Cut a section from the center of a cucumber. Begin to cut the skin from the cucumber flesh but leave the skin at the other end attached.

❺ Cut the cucumber into a series of slices.

❶ Cut off all roots from a washed radish.

❷ Carve a five pointed star on the top of the radish with the point of a knife or a V-shaped carving tool.

❸ Using the same method, make V cuts between the points of the star. Repeat to form the shape of a star emitting light.

❹ Repeat the same procedure over the entire surface of the radish.

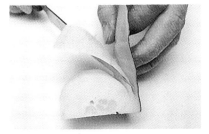

❷ Repeating the same procedure as instruction #1, cut a thin slice of flesh under the slice of skin.

❸ Tuck the ends of the two slices into the crease formed where the skin and the flesh are still connected.

❹ Make a series of cuts into the flesh of the cucumber.

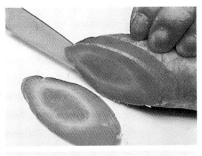

❻ Make a series of diagonal slices on a piece of carrot.

❼ Carve each slice into the shape of a leaf.

❽ Hollow out a space at the center of each leaf.

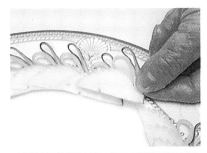

❾ Arrange the cucumber slices on the edge of a plate.

❿ Use three leaves to decorate the cucumber slices; decorate with a piece of cherry.

Improvisation #3

Materials... Radish

❶ Wash a radish and cut off stem.

❷ Slice five pieces from around the center of the radish, forming a five-sided body.

❸ Make a slice on each of the five sides, but do not cut through the radish. This will form the first layer of petals.

❹ Cut out a five pointed star in the center of the radish.

❺ Using the same method, make V cuts in between the points of the star. Repeat the same procedure to form a star imitating light.

❻ Repeat instruction #5 to increase the size of the star.

Improvisation #4

Materials... Daikon

❶ Carve a daikon into a semi-sphere shape 1/8" thick.

❷ Carve a five pointed star on the top center of the semi-sphere, and remove the star.

❸ Using the same method, make V cuts between the points of the star. Repeat the procedure to form a star imitating light.

❹ Use colored dye to enhance this garnish if desired.

Watermelon Rind Design #1

Materials... **Watermelon Rind, Pumpkin**

❶ Select a piece of green watermelon rind.

❷ Sketch a design on the rind and carve along the outline of the design. Remove excess.

❸ Cut a piece of pumpkin flesh into thin slices in the shape of a grain of wheat.

❹ Score curved lines on one side of the pumpkin slice.

❺ Glue the pumpkin piece to the stem formed from the rind. The green and yellow contrast makes an exquisite garnish.

Watermelon Rind Design #2

Materials... **Watermelon Rind, Pumpkin**

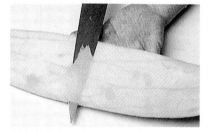

❶ Cut the green portion of the watermelon rind from the white portion of the rind.

❷ Sketch a design on the green rind. Carve along the outline of the design.

❸ Carefully trim the outline of the design. Repeat instructions #1 and #2 with the white portion of the rind.

❹ Carve a piece of pumpkin into a flower design.

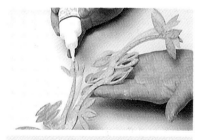

❺ Glue the green and white rind designs together. Then glue the pumpkin flowers to the stems.

Watermelon Rind Design #3

Materials... Watermelon Rind, Pumpkin

❶ Select a piece of watermelon rind with light and dark green shading.

❷ Sketch a design on the rind and carve along the outline of the design.

❸ Cut a piece of pumpkin into slices, and then carve them into cherry blossom shapes.

❹ Glue these cherry blossoms to the stems formed from the watermelon rind.

Watermelon Rind Design #4

Materials... Watermelon Rind, Pumpkin

❶ Cut off the white portion of a watermelon rind, leaving a thin piece of green rind.

❷ Sketch a design on the rind, and carve along the outline of the design.

❸ Cut a piece of pumpkin into thin slices, and then carve the slices into the shapes of flowers.

❹ Glue the flowers to the stems formed by the watermelon rind.

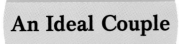

An Ideal Couple

Materials... **Pumpkin, Lotus Root**

❶ Insert a curved-blade knife into the center of the piece of pumpkin. Core out a stick of pumpkin to make the center of the flower.

❷ Select a piece of pumpkin flesh without the rind. Carve the pumpkin piece into a tear-drop shape with notches on each side.

❸ Slice the pumpkin piece into fourteen thin slices crosswise from left to right. These slices form the petals.

❹ Glue the petals onto the carved flower center. Decorate the rest of the plate with lotus roots and broccoli florets.

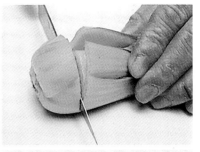

1 Cut the bottom off of a large celery plant, and rinse it with water.

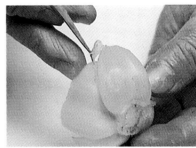

2 Carve petals out of the celery stalks.

3 Keep the root end of the celery in tact while carving the petals.

4 Soak the celery blossoms in cold water to keep them bright green.

Emerald Peony

Materials...
Celery, Orange

New Year's Celebration With Eggplant

Materials... Eggplant

❶ Select a fresh, bright purple eggplant. Cut off both ends. These ends will form the blossoms.

❷ Insert a sharp-pointed knife deep into the flesh of the eggplant, carving out long petals.

❸ Cut slices under the skin "petals" to remove flesh.

❹ Carefully cut out the remaining center flesh. The "petals" should now stand straight up.

❺ Soak the "blossoms" in cold water and lemon juice to prevent discoloration of the flesh. Insert half a maraschino cherry in the center of each blossom.

❶ Peel a fresh carrot, and cut off the top and bottom of the carrot. Carve out thin strips lengthwise on one side of the carrot.

❷ Holding the carrot securely in one hand, use the other hand to cut thin, curved slices crosswise.

❸ Make a small flower center with a piece of taro. Glue the petals to the taro center to form the first layer of petals.

Begonia

Materials...
Carrot, Taro Root

❹ Glue two more layers of petals into the taro to form a begonia blossom.

❺ Decorate the rest of the dish with fresh flowers and oranges to make a beautiful garnish.

Cosmos

Materials... Carrot

❶ From the middle part of a carrot, cut a piece crosswise approximately 3/4 of an inch thick.

❷ Cut around the outside of the carrot piece in a circular direction, forming an umbrella-type shape. Remove the excess.

❸ Score a circle on the flat part of the carrot piece. Deepen the circle.

❹ With a V-shaped carving tool, carve "star-ray" cuts around the circle.

❺ Make "V" cuts between the rays.

❻ Using the same method, make layers of stars. Decorate the rest of the plate with vegetables.

Cymbidium

Materials...
Bamboo Shoots,
Carrot

❶ Select a fresh, large bamboo shoot. Cut off a piece of bamboo at the middle part of the shoot.

❷ Carve the piece of bamboo into petals with the shape of leaves.

❸ Select another piece of bamboo shoot, and carve the piece of bamboo into the form of circular petals.

❹ Cut a small piece of carrot to form the flower center. Glue three long petals to the carrot center to form the first layer of petals.

❺ Glue two pieces of circular petals to the carrot center to form the second layer of petals, forming a cymbidium blossom.

61

❶ Select a fresh gherkin. Cut off both ends of the gherkin into pieces 1 1/4" in length.

❷ Score long and pointed petals into the piece of gherkin.

❸ Cut behind the petals to separate the skin from the flesh of the gherkin. Be careful not to cut off the petals.

Blossoms On Twigs

Materials... Gherkin

❹ Gently remove the center of flesh. Decorate with a piece of maraschino cherry in the center of the flower.

Bell Flower

Materials... Red Chili Pepper

❶ Select a fresh, bright red chili pepper. At the stem end of the pepper, cut off a piece approximately 1 1/4" in length.

❷ Using the tip of a sharp knife, scoop out the seeds.

❸ Using the point of the knife, make even cuts lengthwise on the pepper, leaving the stem end attached.

❹ Gently open up the petals with your hands.

63

White Daisy

Materials...
Daikon, Carrot

❶ Select a fresh white daikon. Cut it into slices of 1/4" thickness. Use a cogwheel shaped cutter to cut out flowers.

❷ Insert a curved-blade carving knife into a piece of carrot to core out a stick. This stick will form the flower center.

❸ Score the carrot stick.

❹ Insert the carrot flower center into the center of the daikon slice. Cut each slice of the daikon cogwheel from the center to the edge, like a spoke.

Orchid

Materials... Daikon, Pumpkin

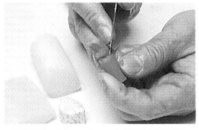

❶ Cut a small piece of pumpkin to form the flower center.

❷ Cut it into two separate pieces. Carve one piece into the shape of a willow leaf, and carve the other piece into the shape of a scallop.

❸ Cut very thin slices crosswise from right to left on each carved daikon piece. Thus, two differently shaped petals are formed.

❹ Glue three pieces of willow leaf petals to the pumpkin center.

❺ Glue two pieces of scallop petals to the center, above the first three petals. Your orchid blossom is now complete.

❻ Soak the blossoms in clean, cold water for two minutes. Use the moistened blossoms as a garnish.

❶ Peel a fresh carrot. Cut off the top and bottom. Carve the piece of carrot into a long tubular heart-shaped piece.

❷ Cut a groove lengthwise at the center top of the piece of carrot. Cut thin, crosswise slices to form petals.

❸ Sort petals by size

❹ Score a small round piece of taro, to be used as the flower center.

Camellia
Goddess Of Mercy

Materials...
Carrot, Taro

❺ Five same-sized carrot slices form one group of petals. Glue the petals to the flower center, forming one layer.

❻ Attach each layer of petals in the order of size, with smaller petals towards the center of the flower.

❼ Place on plate and add greens for an attractive floral garnish.

Carnation

Materials...
Carrot

❶ Peel the carrot and cut off the top and bottom. Cut the carrot into a cylinder with a diameter of 1 1/2".

❷ Carve grooves along the carrot to make a serrated shape.

❸ Cut thin slices crosswise from the carrot cylinder.

❹ Fold each slice in half, and glue down the point at the top center of the slice.

❺ Make a second fold in each slice, and glue down the point as shown.

❻ Five folded carrot slices make up a carnation blossom.

❼ Set the blossom on a light colored plate, or use it to make a solid garnish with other decorations.

❶ Select a fresh carrot. Cut the carrot into a five-sided cylinder.

❷ Cut a groove at the center of each side to form a flower shape.

❸ Using a spiral-like cut, turn the knife two times around the vegetable.

Cherry Blossom
Greeting The New Year

Materials...Carrot, Black Sesame Seeds

❺ Place black sesame seeds in the center of the cherry blossom with a bamboo stick.

❹ Form into cherry blossom.

❶ Select a fresh piece of taro root. Carve it into a stick with a diameter of approximately 1/2 inch.

❷ Cut diagonally at a 45 degree angle crosswise to form a long and thin slice by making a "spiral cut."

❸ To make a blossom, "roll up" three times by turning the taro stick with one hand while holding the knife in the other hand.

❹ Decorate with small pieces of carrot at the center of the flower.

Fleur-De-Lis

Materials... Taro Root, Carrot

❶ Insert a curved-blade knife into the center of the carrot to core out a stick to be used as the flower's center. Peel a taro root.

❷ Cut the root into two pieces. Carve one piece into a long willow leaf shape, and carve the other piece into a scallop shape.

❸ Cut both carved root pieces crosswise into very thin slices. This will form two differently shaped petals.

❹ Glue three long petals to the carrot center, and glue three pieces of scalloped shaped petals above the first layer of long petals. Make a deep groove into the carrot stick.

Orchid

Materials... Taro, Pumpkin, Carrot

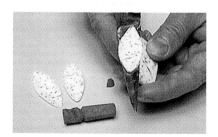

❶ Select a fresh taro. Carve a piece of taro into a willow leaf shape.

❷ Select a fresh, brightly colored pumpkin, and carve a piece of the pumpkin flesh into a scallop shape.

❸ Slice the carved piece of pumpkin into thin curved slices, to form the orchid's golden petals.

❹ Using the same method as step 3, cut the carved piece of taro into thin curved slices. Core out a carrot to be used as the flower's center.

❺ Glue three taro petals around the center, then glue three pumpkin petals above the first layer of taro petals, alternating the position of the petals between layers.

❻ Soak the blossom in cold water for a few minutes.

Chrysanthemum

Materials... Orange

❶ Select a fresh, brightly colored orange. Cut the orange into halves crosswise. Cut a slice off the top end of each piece of the orange.

❷ Cut the orange slices to form multipointed stars as shown in the photograph.

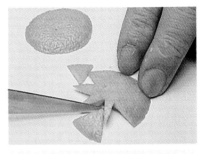

❸ Cut off the white portion (orange pith) of the stars, keeping the skin of the orange in tact.

❹ Glue three stars together, one on top of the other, to form a chrysanthemum.

Snow Lotus

Materials... Onion, Carrot

❶ Select a fresh white onion. Cut the onion in half lengthwise. Cut each half lengthwise into three even slices.

❷ Separate each layer of the onion slices, and sort the pieces by size.

❸ Use a small piece of carrot as the flower's center; glue the petals onto it.

❹ Five same-sized onion pieces make up one layer of petals. Arrange each layer so that the smaller sized petals are placed closer to the flower's center.

Winter Plum Blossom

Materials... Daikon, Carrot

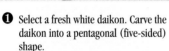

❶ Select a fresh white daikon. Carve the daikon into a pentagonal (five-sided) shape.

❷ Cut a groove at the center of each of the five sides, lengthwise. Round out the shape of the petals.

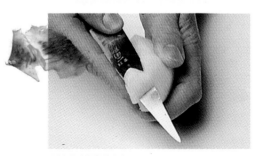

❸ Holding the daikon with one hand, use the other hand to cut the daikon at a 45 degree angle. Roll up three times to form the petals.

❹ Gently form the petals by hand. Decorate with little pieces of carrot at the flower's center. Glue the blossoms onto plum branches.

❷ Cut out the shape of the fish. Remove and save excess pumpkin.

❸ Cut out the fins and tail.

❹ Trim the fins and tail. Use a V-shaped carving tool to carve grooves on both sides of the fins and tail.

Angel Fish

Materials... **Pumpkin**

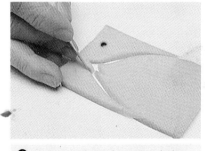

❶ Peel a pumpkin and cut it into thick slices. Using the point of a knife, score the shape of an angel fish on the pumpkin slice.

❺ Use extra pieces of pumpkin to form two large whiskers. Attach them under the gills. Attach fins on each side of the fish. Add eyes.

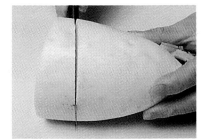

❶ Select a fresh, white daikon. Cut a wedge-shaped piece at an angle crosswise. This piece will form the body of the swan.

❺ Roll a curved shaped carving tool under the beak to form the jowl. The head of the swan is now complete.

Swan

Materials... Daikon, Carrot

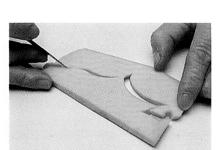

❶ Select a fresh pumpkin with gold-colored flesh. Cut the pumpkin into thick slices. Using the point of a knife, score the fins of a fish.

❷ Using the point of a knife, cut out the rest of the fish.

Tuna Fish

Materials... **Pumpkin, Taro Root**

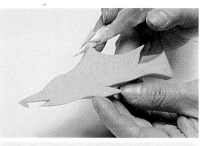

❸ Carve straight lines on the fins of the back and stomach of the fish.

❹ Carve a fan-shaped tail carefully . Next, carve a taro root to form waves. Set the fish and waves on broccoli florets.

❷ Use the narrower part of the wedge for the head of the swan. Cut a small triangle on the top right part of the wedge.

❸ Carve a beak-shaped piece of carrot, and attach it to the indentation formed as shown in #2.

❹ Shape a neck behind the head. Cut a small triangle on the other side of the wedge to form the tail.

❻ Trim the neck and the chest of the swan into a smooth shape.

❼ Use a curved-blade carving tool to carefully cut out a pair of "fluttering" wings.

❽ Trim the rest of the body of the swan so that it is smooth.

❾ Carve another swan, one with flat (not fluttering) wings.

❿ Carefully carve feathers on both sets of wings. Decorate with broccoli florets and lettuce.

❶ Select a fresh white daikon. Cut a wedge shaped piece crosswise at an angle. This piece will form the body of the goose.

❺ Form a neck and stomach.

Wild Goose

Materials...Daikon, Durian, Pumpkin

Mermaid

Materials... Pumpkin, Scallions, Rambutan

❶ Select fresh scallions and cut off the white portion. Cut off the ends of the leaves at an angle.

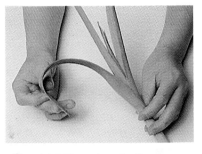

❷ Lightly fold over the ends of leaves to create a tree-like shape.

❸ Score the outline of a mermaid on the rind of a pumpkin, and begin to cut the figure out.

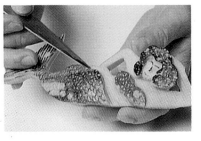

❹ Etch the face and details of the body onto the rind.

❺ Carve the tail, and use a curved-blade carving tool to form scales. Form trees with scallions, and decorate with rambutan.

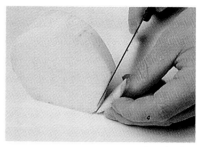

❷ Use the narrower part of the wedge to form the head of the goose. Cut a small piece off this end. Cut the bottom of the wedge flat.

❸ Carve a piece of pumpkin into a beak, and attach the beak where you cut off the small piece in step #**2**.

❹ Form the back of a goose by cutting back from the head.

❻ Use another piece of daikon to carve a pair of wings.

❼ Trim the wing piece, and cut feathers into each side of the piece.

❽ Cut the wing piece in half.

❾ Trim the wings into the proper shape.

❿ Attach the wings to the body of the goose. Decorate with a durian.

❶ Cut a piece of daikon in half lengthwise.

❷ Cut a pumpkin to form the beak. Use the rind as a feather. Cut a carrot to form a cap for the crane's head.

❸ Carve one of the daikon pieces to form the outline of a crane.

❹ Carve the breast and stomach of the crane.

Cranes Mean Longevity

Materials... **Daikon, Pumpkin, Carrot**

❺ Attach the beak, carrot top, and breast feather to the body of the crane with glue.

❻ Using a curved-blade carving tool, carve feathers into the crane's entire body.

❼ Use a magic marker to dot skewers, making them resemble a crane's legs.

❽ Insert the legs into the crane body.

❾ Using the other half of the daikon, cut two thin slices to form the wings.

❿ Carefully cut feathers onto the wings.

⓫ Attach the wings to the body of the crane with glue.

❶ From a piece of taro, carve out the head of a dragon.

❷ Carve the face.

❸ Carefully carve whiskers.

❹ Carve the neck of the dragon.

Dragons Dictate Fortune

Materials...
Taro Root

❺ Using a curved-blade carving tool, carve scales onto the neck.

❻ Carve the rest of the dragon's body so that it suits the head and neck.

❼ Use four other small pieces of taro to carve into claws with scales.

❽ Using a sharp-pointed knife, complete carving the claws.

❾ Cut a piece of taro to form the tail of the dragon.

❿ Carve fins and the tail.

⓫ Attach the head, tail, and body with glue.

Cardinals

Materials... Carrot

Using pieces of ginger root, build a background for the garnish.

Decorate with azalea leaves, flowers made from chili peppers (see page 63) and asparagus fern.

❶ Peel a fresh carrot. Cut off the top and bottom of the carrot, leaving a large piece to make into the bird.

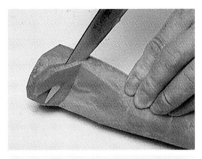

❷ As shown in the photograph, cut a wedge in the side of the piece of carrot. This wedge will be used to form the head of the bird.

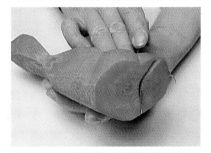

❸ At the other end of the carrot, cut a wedge on each side, to shape into the tail of the bird.

❹ Cut the part between the head and tail to form the chest of the bird.

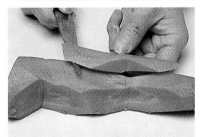

❺ Carve the chest area so that it becomes smooth.

❻ Carve a beak and a jaw on the head. Trim the area so that the shape flows continuously between the head and the jaw.

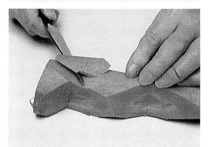

❼ Cut diagonally under the tail, and shape the tail feathers and both legs of the bird.

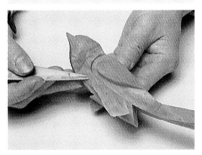

❽ Score the wings approximately 1/2" behind the head.

❾ Using a curved-blade carving tool, cut out layers of feathers in the wings.

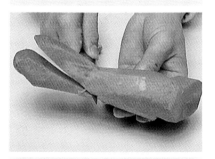

❿ Cut another piece of carrot and carve it into the shape of a fluttering wing.

⓫ Using a curved-blade carving tool, carve and trim the fluttering wing.

⓬ Attach the wings to the body of the birds. Make one bird with fluttering wings, and one bird with flat wings.

Flower Cart

Materials... Taro Root, Carrot

❶ Cut a taro crosswise to form slices 1/2 inch thick. Shape the slices into disks about 2 1/2 inches in diameter.

❷ Using a curved-blade carving tool, scoop out five holes on the disks, forming the cart's wheels.

❸ Carve a small piece of carrot into a disk, and attach it at the center of the taro wheel.

❹ Along the outer side of the wheel, carve a circle to form the rim of the wheel.

❺ Carve a long piece of taro into a spoon-like shape. This piece will form the body of the cart.

❻ Carve the tail end of the cart into a spiral shape.

❼ Attach one wheel to each side of the cart with toothpicks. Set a carved flower on the cart.

Materials...
Taro Root, Pumkin

❶ Select a piece of taro
that has been peeled and
washed. Carve out the shape
of a monkey in the taro.

❷ Carve a head and two legs.

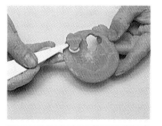

❸ Scoop out a piece of taro
where the monkey face will
be located. Carve a monkey
face out of a slice of carrot.

❹ Insert the piece of monkey
face into the proper spot on
the taro.

❺ Carve eyes and ears for the
completed head.

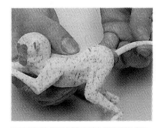

❻ Cut another piece of taro
into a long, thin tail.
Attach the tail at the end of
the body.

❼ Trim the chest and stomach
areas to complete the
monkey.

Beautiful Phoenix

Materials... Taro Root

❶ Select a large piece of fresh taro. Cut out the shape of a phoenix.

❷ Cut layers of neck feathers towards the top of the carving.

❸ Carve feathers on the body with a small curved-blade carving tool.

❹ Select another piece of taro. Score a sketch of claws using a sharp-pointed knife.

❺ After finishing carving the claws, attach them to the body of the phoenix.

❻ Cut long, thin slices of taro about 6 inches in length. Cut indentations on both sides to form the tail.

❼ Carve tail feathers carefully. The length of the tail depends upon your design.

❽ Attach the tail onto the body of the phoenix with glue. You have now completed the body of the phoenix.

❾ Cut two large pieces of taro to form wings.

❿ Complete carving wings by forming layers of feathers.

⓫ Using a V-shaped carving tool, carve solid feathers into the wings.

⓬ Attach both wings to the body of the phoenix.

Heroic Eagles

Materials... Taro Root

❶ Sketch an eagle shape on a piece of taro root, using a curved-blade carving tool. Carve the body of the eagle.

❷ Carve out the tail feathers.

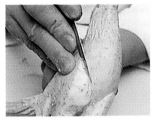

❸ Carve two legs under the stomach of the bird.

❹ Shape a sharp beak at the top part of the head.

❺ The method of cutting wings is the same as the phoenix on page 87 numbers 9-11.

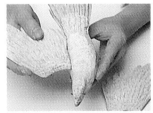

❻ Attach one wing on each side of the eagle.

❼ Look over the bird, trimming any areas which need to be smoothed out.

Combination Of Four Winds

Combination Of Four Winds

Materials... Orange, Watermelon Rind, Mango, Kiwi

❶ Select two fresh, same-sized oranges with a thin smooth skin. Cut the top off each orange, on the side with the stem.

❷ On each orange, make a thin slice crosswise, and at the end, cut according to instruction 1. Cut only as far as the center of the orange.

❸ On the other side of the same orange, make the same cut as you did according to instruction 2 above. Do not cut through the orange.

❹ Pull the two cut ends of the slice together, and glue them in the center. Cut out the flesh of the orange under the joined slice, forming the handle.

Firedragon Melon

Materials...
Firedragon Melon

Firedragon is a hot fruit, and should be eaten in combination with chilled fruits. Cut into wedges and arrange with greens for a colorful garnish.

Rambutan

Materials... Rambutan

❶ Wash a rambutan. Cut the rind around the middle with the point of a knife.

❷ Gently open the rind with the knife-point, revealing the white flesh inside.

❸ To eat, scoop out the flesh with a spoon.

Watermelon Dragon

Materials... Watermelon

❶ Select a fresh, large watermelon with red flesh. Cut a long, thin slice lengthwise. Be careful to keep the flesh in tact when slicing.

❷ Using the point of a knife, gently cut the outline of a dragon head at the top of the slice.

❸ Cut out the shape of horns and the back of a dragon.

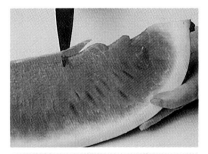

❹ Cut away a piece of flesh to form the tail of the dragon.

❺ Trim each part of the dragon's body. The finished product will be a dragon formed from one slice of watermelon.

Southern Style Durian

Materials... Durian

❶ Using a sturdy knife, cut away part of the durian's hard rind.

❷ Lift the rind off the durian. Serve chilled with chunks of durian and ice cubes set on top of the open fruit.

Mango

Materials... Mango

❶ Wash a mango. Cut two pieces lengthwise from each side.

❷ Cut the pieces crosswise into thick slices, leaving the skin attached.

❸ Peel the center part of the mango containing the pit, and cut it into a heart shape.

Apple Happiness

Materials... Apple

❶ Wash a fresh apple. Using the point of a knife, cut out the center part of the apple with the stem.

❷ Cut the apple into six even-sized pieces. Place the pieces on a plate, with one piece leaning on the next.

❸ Select another apple with an elongated shape. Insert the point of the knife into the middle of apple, forming V-cuts around the center of the fruit.

❹ Extend the V-cuts through the apple so that you can separate it into two pieces with your hands.

❺ Place a maraschino cherry on the top of each half of the apple, and arrange with other apple slices as shown.

93

❶ Select a fresh, large watermelon with red flesh. Cut it lengthwise into six pieces, and use one piece.

❷ Cut the rind off the piece of melon, and slice the flesh crosswise into thick slices.

❸ Pick up the slices, with the aid of a knife and lightly set them on a diagonal with the other fruits.

Combination Of Five Fruits

*Materials...*Watermelon, Kiwi, Papaya, Orange, Rambutan

Papaya Pagoda

Materials... Papaya, Kiwi

❶ Cut a papaya lengthwise into six pieces. Remove the seeds from one of the pieces.

❷ Peel the papaya. Score intersecting lines on the surface and cut the end of the piece into a V-shape.

❸ Place the pagoda-like papaya piece in the center of a plate. Decorate with kiwi and papaya.

❶ Divide an orange into six slices, but do not cut all the way through the skin. Divide another orange into six slices, this time cutting all the way through.

❷ Begin to cut the skin from a slice of orange but stop before reaching the other end of the orange, leaving the last third of skin intact and attached to the flesh.

❸ Starting from the end where the skin is attached, cut a diagonal slice lengthwise towards the middle of the detached skin. Stop before reaching the end of the skin.

❹ Take the tip of the cut skin (right where you began your diagonal slice) and prop it up against the flesh of the orange, as shown.

❶ Cut the skin off of orange slices, leaving the last third of the skin attached.

❷ Make two diagonal cuts lengthwise, from the edge to the center, on the separated skin. Do not bring the two cuts together to form a V.

❸ Fold the separated skin into the crease, where the skin is still attached to the orange.

Double Flavor Appetizer #2

Materials...Orange, Strawberry

Melon And Fruit Appetizer

Materials... Apples, Watermelon

❶ Sketch an outline of a mouse on the watermelon rind. Use a stencil of the design as a guide.

❷ Etch out the picture, and then carve the shape out of the rind.

❸ Another piece of watermelon rind is the base, attach the carving with toothpicks.

Chinese Banana Boat

Materials... Banana, Apple

❶ Insert a knife through the center of a peeled banana, forming a slit in the middle.

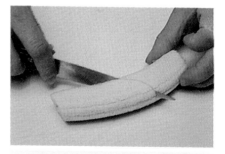

❷ Make a diagonal cuts crosswise at the right end of the slit. Cut only to down to the slit, and do not cut through the banana.

❸ Turn the banana over and make a diagonal cut on the left end of the slit in the same fashion. Slide the banana open with your hands.

❹ Set the pieces of banana on a fruit tray or cup. Decorate with other fruits.

❶ Wash and peel a kiwi. Cut off the ends.

❷ Divide the kiwi lengthwise into six pieces.

❸ For variety, cut a kiwi in half lengthwise. Use a spoon, scoop out the inside to eat.

Home Style Kiwi Cutting

Materials... Kiwi

Lovely Tomato

Materials... Honeydew, Tomatos

❶ Using a U-shaped carving tool, cut off the top 1/3 of the melon, forming a cup with fancy edges.

❷ Use toothpicks, to attach a design (carved from watermelon rind) to the side of the melon cup.

❸ Set "double slices" of cucumber (pg.17) around a plate. Fill the melon cup with cherry tomatoes.

Long Lasting Love

Materials... Cantalope

❶ Make a slightly sloping cut lengthwise near the middle of a cantaloupe. Then make another parallel cut, forming the handles of a basket.

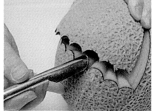

❷ Make a series of cuts with a U-shaped tool around center of the cantaloupe. Repeat step 2 with the second, parallel cut.

❸ Remove the excess pieces of flesh under the handle, forming a basket.

❹ Cut out a triangle on each side of the handle near the its base, using a U-shaped carving tool and a knife.

❺ Using a U-shaped carving tool or a melon baler, scoop out the inside of the basket.

❻ Using a U-shaped carving tool, core out holes just under the laced edge of the basket.

❼ Cut the rind of each slice, leaving the last third intact, with the rind attached to the flesh.

❽ Cut out leaf-like shapes on the separated part of the rind, leaving the attached rind with a V-shape.

Home Sweet Home

Materials... Watermelon, Maraschino Cherry, Kiwi, Honeydew

❶ Cut a yellow honeydew lengthwise into eight slices. Cut a kiwi into thick slices, and decorate with maraschino cherries.

❷ Cut a V-shape on the rind of the melon. In the alternative, create your own design by carving the rind.

❸ Begin to cut the rind, but stop before reaching the other end. Leave the other end of the rind attached to the flesh.

❹ Remove excess rind.

❺ Cut the flesh of a watermelon into curved slices. Set the watermelon around the center of a white plate.

Paradise Island

*Materials...*Watermelon, Lime, Maraschino Cherries

❶ Cut the middle part of a small watermelon crosswise into one inch thick slices. Carve a series of peaks into the flesh.

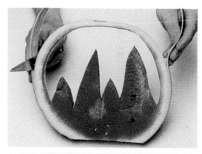

❷ Begin to cut the green part of the rind off the watermelon, but stop half way. Carve the separated rind into rabbit-ear shapes.

❸ Cut a lime crosswise into "double slices" (see page 17). Create lime slices in three different sizes by slicing the entire lime.

❹ Place the largest slice of lime flat, and then attach second and third smaller slices on top of it with a toothpick.

❺ Place a maraschino cherry on top of the lime flower. Add these lime flowers to decorate the fruit plate.

Phoenix Boat

Materials... Yellow Honeydew Melon, Watermelon

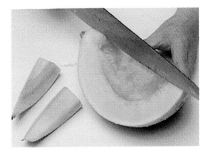

❶ Select a fresh yellow honeydew melon, and cut it lengthwise into long slices.

❷ On each slice, cut the shape of a leaf, or your own design, onto the rind. Remove the excess rind.

❸ Begin to cut the rind, but stop before reaching the other end. Leave the other end of the rind attached to the flesh.

❹ Follow instruction #3 with a slice of watermelon. Slice the opened rind into two layers. Fold the inner slice into the crease.

❺ Cut and fold back the outer layer of the watermelon rind as shown.

Pineapple Boat

Materials... Pineapple

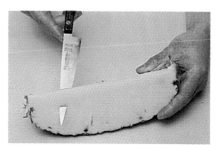

❶ Using one quarter of a pineapple, cut a slit lengthwise in the pineapple flesh just below the top of the wedge.

❷ Make the same slit at the bottom of the wedge, and then connect the two slits on each end of the pineapple. Remove the flesh between the two slits.

❸ Cut the removed piece of flesh into thick slices.

❹ Insert the slices back into the hole in the pineapple slice. For an extra special touch, slide out each slice in the opposite direction.

Chef's Watermelon

Materials...
Watermelon

❶ Cut a watermelon into slices lengthwise. Using half a slice, carve the ridge of flesh into a curved design.

❷ Cut off a piece of flesh near the white part of the rind. This will from a crease that will be used in instruction #5. Trim a flat bottom.

❸ Cut the rind into two layers. Stop before reaching the other end of the rind, keeping the bottom part intact and attached to the flesh.

❹ Make two cuts in each layer of the separated part of the rind, as shown.

❺ Gently fold the separated inner layer of rind into the crease.

❶ Trim each ridge of a star fruit.

❷ Cut the star fruit in half lengthwise.

❸ Cut each half crosswise into slices. Set the slices on a plate with the other fruit.

A Gathering Of The Splendid & Beautiful

Materials... Star Fruit

Select colorful fruit to surround the star fruit.

A Small Dish Of Three Fruits

*Materials...*Mango, Apple, Orange

Add greens for color and serve fruits in a small pedestal dish.

❶ Cut two pieces of flesh lengthwise from a mango.

❷ Cut an apple lengthwise into eight pieces. Carve a design into the skin of each slice.

❸ Cut a leaf shape in the carved design. (See #2) Arrange apple and orange slices with pieces of mango.

Happiness

Materials... Honeydew Melon, Apples

The Sun And The Moon

Materials... Yellow Honeydew Melon

❶ Cut a yellow honeydew melon lengthwise into eight slices. Carve a design on the rind of each slice.

❷ Begin to cut the rind off the slices, but stop before reaching the other end. Leave the other end of the rind attached to the flesh.

❸ Hollow out the design on each slice. Carve a design on the rind of a watermelon and attach the design to complete the garnish.

❶ Cut a honeydew melon lengthwise into six slices. Remove the seeds.

❷ Cut off the sharp ends of each melon slice, forming a semi-circle shape.

❸ Begin to cut the rind off the slices of honeydew, but stop before reaching the other end. Leave the other end of the rind attached to the flesh.

❹ Made two diagonal cuts on the detached rind of the melon slices as shown.

❺ Tuck the end of the detached rind into the crease when the rind joins the flesh.

❻ Cut an apple lengthwise into six slices. Remove the seeds and stems from each piece.

❼ Be careful not to cut too much flesh off the apple.

❽ Score the shape of leaves in the skin of the apple, and remove the excess skin.

❾ Carve a design in the center of each leaf cut into the apple skin.

The Sun And The Moon

Materials... Yellow Honeydew Melon

Fortune Has Descended Upon Our Home

Materials...
Apples,
Honeydew Melon

❶ Cut an apple lengthwise into four slices. Cut off the seeds and stems from each slice.

❷ Cut a series of V-shaped wedges from apple.

❸ Fan the V-shaped slices as shown.

❹ Partially cut the rind from honeydew slices. Leave the end attached. Cut the detached rind into 2 layers.

❺ Tuck the top layer of the detached rind into the crease formed by the rind attached to the flesh.

❻ Tuck the bottom layer of the detached rind into the crease, as shown.

Improvisation

Materials... Watermelon

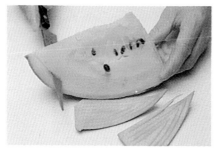

❶ Cut the rind off a slice of watermelon, and then cut the flesh into a design of your own creation.

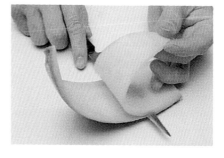

❷ Separate the white section of the rind.

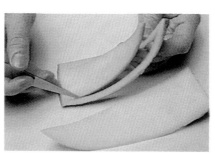

❸ Starting at the pointed end, carve a V-shape into the green part of the rind. Do not cut all the way to the end of the rind.

❹ Cut successive V-shaped cuts inside the first V-shaped cut you made according to instruction #3.

Together Forever

Materials... Watermelon

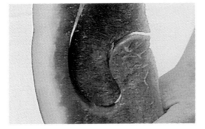

❶ Slice a watermelon lengthwise, and cut a flat bottom. Carve the shape of a swan into the flesh of the watermelon slice.

❷ Cut the flesh and rind into the shape of swan tail feathers.

❸ Carve the shape of the swan into the flesh. You may use a stencil as a guide to form this shape.

❹ Carve the rind of another watermelon slice into the shape of a pine tree for decoration.

❺ Complete carving the rind of the watermelon into the pine tree shape as shown.

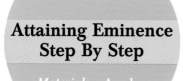

**Attaining Eminence
Step By Step**

Materials... Apples

❶ Cut an apple in half lengthwise.

❷ Cut one of the halves into four slices lengthwise.

❸ Score a leaf shape into the skin of an apple slice.

❹ Cut the excess off around and under the leaf shape on the apple slice. See page 103 for instructions for the Pineapple Boat.

Reunion

Materials... Honeydew, Star Fruit

❶ Insert a sharp-pointed knife into the side of the honeydew. Cut V-shaped petals around the side of a honeydew melon.

❷ On every V-shaped petal formed according to instruction #1, cut the rind back from the flesh to form the shape of lotus flower's petals.

❸ A close-up of the lotus flower blossom.

❹ Cut a cleaned star fruit crosswise into slices. Decorate with a kiwi slice and maraschino cherry half on top.

The Five Ethnic Groups Of China

Materials... Mangosteen

❶ Score a 1/2 inch slit around the center of the mangosteen, so that the rind can be opened.

❷ Be careful while scoring the rind to avoid injuring the flesh.

❸ Gently remove the stem of the mangosteen, revealing the bright white flesh inside.

❹ Use a teaspoon to scoop out the flesh for eating.

Living And Playing Together In Childhood

Materials... Watermelon

❶ Cut a small watermelon lengthwise into slices, and cut off the rind.

❷ Carve the flesh of the watermelon into a crescent shape. See page 100 for yellow melon garnishes.

Four Fruit Appetizer

Materials... Apple, Cherries, Watermelon, Firedragon

❶ Cut a watermelon with yellow flesh into triangle shapes.

❷ Cut a firedragon melon into slices lengthwise. Peel the slices.

❸ Cut a flat base at the end of each slice of firedragon melon so that you can place each slice standing up.

❶ Carve out a design on the rind of a watermelon. Cut the flesh of a watermelon into random-sized blocks.

❷ See page 108 for directions for cutting the yellow apple.

❸ Cut the apple lengthwise into slices. Trim the slices into leaf-like shapes.

Bamboo Reports Everything Is Well

*Materials...*Watermelon, Apple

Colorful Exuberance

Materials... Firedragon

❶ Cut a firedragon melon lengthwise into slices.

❷ Cut the rind off the slices of the firedragon melon.

❸ Use the colorful rind as decoration.

Aim High

Materials... Watermelon, Orange

❶ Begin to cut the rind off slices of watermelon, but stop before reaching the other end, leaving the last third attached to the flesh. Cut out the white portion of the rind.

❷ Cut a diagonal slice lengthwise towards the middle of the detached rind. Stop before reaching the end. Prop the tip of the cut rind against the flesh.

❸ Use the same shown in instructions #1-2 on an orange. Arrange each type of fruit into one row to make this colorful garnish.

❶ Cut a pineapple lengthwise into long slices. Cut the rind off the pineapple slices.

❷ Cut the core off one of the slices, and then cut the slice crosswise into thick pieces.

❸ Using the side of a knife, slightly separate the slices of pineapple, and set them on the plate.

❹ See page 28 for directions for preparing the honeydew garnish.

Ode To Happiness

Materials... Watermelon, Orange

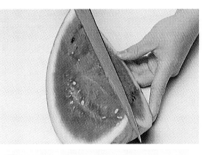

❶ Cut a fresh watermelon lengthwise into slices. Be careful to keep the watermelon flesh intact while cutting.

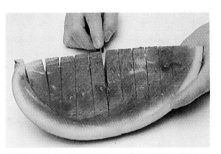

❷ Starting from one end, make a cut to separate the flesh from the rind. Then cut the flesh crosswise into thick slices. Slide out each slice in the opposite direction.

❸ Begin to cut the rind off slices of an orange, but stop before reaching the other end, leaving the last third attached to the flesh.

❹ Cut a diagonal slice lengthwise towards the middle of the detached rind. Stop before reaching the end. Prop the tip of the cut rind against the flesh.

Blooming Of The Fruit Tree

Materials...
Orange, Apple

❶ Cut a V-shape into the skin at the center of an orange slice. Hold the orange slice so that the point of the V points to the left.

❷ Starting at the right side of the orange, begin to cut the skin from the orange slice, but stop before reaching the other end.

❸ Leave the last third of skin intact and attached to the flesh. Prop the point of the rind against the flesh of the orange.

❹ Cut a fresh apple lengthwise into slices. Score a design on the skin of each slice.

❺ Carve a design into each slice, and remove the excess skin. Arrange the garnish as shown.

Competition In Beauty

Materials...
Yellow Melon

❶ Begin to cut the skin from an orange slice, but stop before reaching the end. Leave the last third of skin attached. Starting at an edge of the skin on the end where the skin is still attached, make six slices towards the detached skin. Stop before reaching the end. Cut the six slices away from the attached rind, so that they fan out into a broom shape. Be sure that some skin still remains attached to the flesh. Prop the broom shape up against the flesh.

Use the same method on page 108 to create the "apple pagoda".

Suspicion

Materials...
Orange

❶ Cut a melon lengthwise. Begin to cut the flesh, but stop before reaching the other end. Leave the last third of the skin attached. Starting at the end of the slice where the rind has been detached, cut a V-shape into the rind so that the point of the V points to the end of the slice where the rind is still attached. Prop the point against the flesh.

Decorate with fruit and vegetables to emphasize the color.

❷ Begin to cut the skin from the slice, but stop before reaching the other end, leaving the last third of skin attached to the flesh.

❸ Tuck the end of the rind into the crease formed by the attached part of the skin.

❹ Carve the rind of a watermelon slice into the shape of leaves. Cut the flesh into pieces.

A Pillar Supporting Heaven

Materials... Orange, Watermelon

❶ Cut an orange into thin slices lengthwise.

❺ Place layers of fruits on tiered dishes to complete the garnish.

The Glorious Imperial Palace

Materials... Pineapple, Watermelon, Honeydew Melon

❶ Cut a slice out of the middle of a pineapple lengthwise. Cut a slice off the bottom.

❷ Begin to cut the rind off a slice of watermelon, but stop before reaching the other end, leaving the other end of the rind attached.

❸ Cut the detached rind into two layers. Cut from the edge of the rind in towards the center of the slice.

❹ Starting towards the end of the slice where the rind is still attached, make a V-shaped cut into the green part of the rind.

❺ Tuck the white portion of the slice into the crease formed by the attached part of rind.

❻ Trim the flesh into a crescent shape. Prop the two points of the V formed as shown in instruction #4.

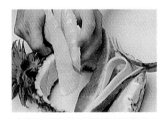

❼ Slice the pineapple flesh into random-sized pieces as shown in instruction #1.

❽ See page 102 for instructions for decorating the honeydew melon.

Combination Of Three Fruits

Materials... Apple, Watermelon, Cherries

❶ Cut a fresh apple lengthwise into slices.

❷ Remove the seeds, but leave as much flesh on as possible.

❸ Slice towards the skin, cut the apple in half lengthwise, but leave the skin attached at the center of the slice.

❹ Open the apple slice to form a butterfly.

❺ Cut a watermelon lengthwise into slices.

❻ Cut the rind away from the flesh. Carve the flesh into the design of your choice.

❼ Cut a V-shape in the center of the rind. Hold the rind so that point of the V-shape points to the right.

❽ See pg. 120 to separate the melon rind. Prop the point of the V-shaped cut against the white part of the rind.

Relationship With Happiness

Materials... Orange, Yellow Honey Melon

❶ Cut the skin off of orange slices, leaving the last third of the skin attached.

❷ Make two diagonal incisions lengthwise from the edge to the center on the separated skin, without bringing the two incisions together to form a V.

❸ Fold the separated skin over into the crease where the skin is still attached to the orange. Bunny ears will pop out.

❹ Cut a yellow honey melon into long slices. Score the shape of leaves into the rind of a melon slice.

❺ Carve out the leaf shapes from the rind.

HOW TO GARNISH / COMO CREAR DECORACIONES CULINARIAS *By Harvey Rosen*

"How To Garnish/Como Crear Decoraciones Culinarias" is more than just the most useful and informative book about food garnishing. It's also the easiest to learn from, because it combines easy-to-follow instructions with illustrations that show exactly what to do.
No guesswork involved; everything you need to know is right here. This is a washable, hard-cover book.

More than twenty full-color photographs and over two hundred illustrations depicting a variety of exquisite arrangements are included. Available with 5 Garnishing Tools: Corrugated Garnishing Blade, Spiral Slicer, Paring Knife, Food Decorator and Twin Curl Cutter.

ISBN:0-939763-09-5 #4433 How To Garnish (Book Only)
ISBN:0-939763-10-9 #4431 How To Garnish (Book/Tools)
ISBN:0-939763-05-2 #4440 Como Crear Decoraciones Culinarias (Book Only)
ISBN:0-939763-08-7 #4441 Como Crear Decoraciones Culinarias (Book/Tools)

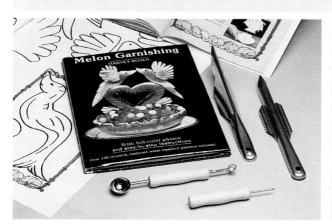

MELON GARNISHING *By Harvey Rosen*

"Melon Garnishing", provides easy-to-follow step-by-step instructions that make the preparation of melons into a pleasurable, creative undertaking. Included with the book are over 100 full-size stencils and four beautifully designed tools. The tools were designed to save time and give melon garnishes a professional flair. The V-Decorator, U-Decorator, Melon Baller and Sketching Tool are precisely crafted from heavy-gauge stainless steel and imported hardwoods.

ISBN:0-9612572-3-7 #4434 Melon Garnishing (Book Only)
ISBN:0-9612572-4-5 #4433 Melon Garnishing (Book/Tools)

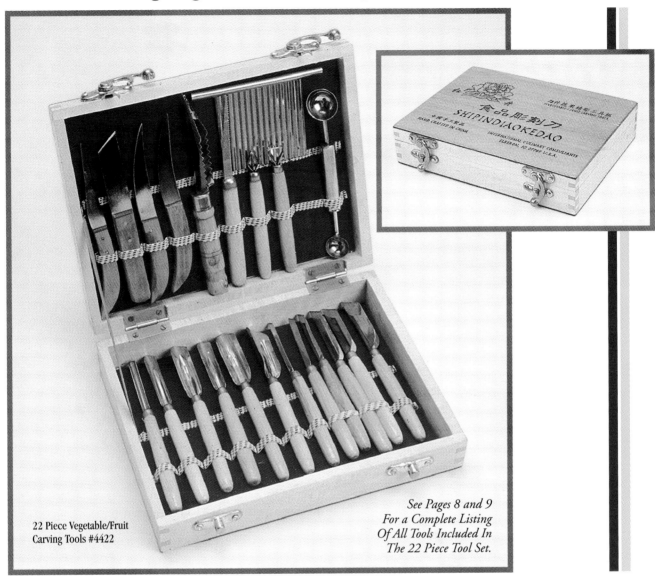

22 Piece Vegetable/Fruit
Carving Tools #4422

*See Pages 8 and 9
For a Complete Listing
Of All Tools Included In
The 22 Piece Tool Set.*

VEGETABLE AND FRUIT DESIGN CUTTERS

*These Unique, Long Life
Design Cutters
Are Hand-Crafted
From Heavy Guage
Stainless Steel.*

*(See Page 12 For Instructions and
Page 22 For a Suggested Plate Decoration.)*

Vegetable
and Fruit Design
Cutters #4450

80 Piece Vegetable/Fruit
Carving Tools #4480

*See Pages 8 and 9
For a Complete Listing
Of All Tools Included In
The 80 Piece Tool Set.*

*These tools are practical as well as good-looking.
With high quality stainless steel and hardwood construction
and ergonomically designed contours, they mold to your hand.
The tools are wedged in their own niche in the
plush red lining of their individually crafted
lacquered hardwood carrying case.*

APPLE GARNISHING *By Harvey Rosen*

Mouth-watering, full-color photos and step-by-step illustrations set the stage for taste-tempting creations that flow from the gifted hands of chef/author Harvey Rosen. This book incorporates a wealth of historical, variety and recipe information about apples....it's almost a mini-apple encyclopedia! Profusely illustrated with dozens of full-color photographs of birds, animals, fish and other creations that can be carved from apples, with easy-to-follow carving instructions. Majestic in its scope and presentation, the book is a visual treat and a delightfully useful guide to the creation of unique table decorations.

HOW TO GARNISH
Video *By Harvey Rosen*

The art of food garnishing is now as easy as turning on your TV/VCR and playing this delightful video. Chef Harvey, internationally respected in the culinary field, leads you step-by-step to a new skill that you'll enjoy putting to use. Chef Harvey is mesmerizing. His unique blend of clever remarks, amusing anecdotes and witty approach to garnishing makes learning this craft easy and fun. You'll learn how to use the specialized garnishing tools and how to create the beautiful designs. You'll learn in a new way that guarantees success. Chef Harvey shows you the way, step-by-step, item-by-item, right before your eyes. This 73 minute video will be the best food preparation investment you'll every make.

ISBN:0-939763-03-6 #4501 IN ENGLISH
ISBN:0-939763-03-4 #4502 IN SPANISH

4-APPLE GARNISHING TOOLS

The four Apple Garnishing tools are Corrugated Apple Wedger, Apple Corer, Thumb Decorator/Peeler, and Paring Knife.

ISBN:0-96112572-8-8 #4437 APPLE GARNISHING (Book Only)
ISBN:0-96112572-4-5 #4434 APPLE GARNISHING (Book/Tools)

**6-Piece
Stainless Steel
CARVING SET**
12 Cutting Edges
• 6- "V" Cutters
• 6- "U" Cutters
#4416

For More Information On Any Item Listed In This Book Contact:
INTERNATIONAL CULINARY CONSULTANTS
Post Office Box 2202 • Elberon, New Jersey 07740 U.S.A.
E-mail: chefharvey@chefharvey.com • Web Site: http://www.chefharvey.com